DATE DUE

Put Beginning Readers on the Right Track with
ALL ABOARD READING™

The All Aboard Reading series is especially designed for beginning readers. Written by noted authors and illustrated in full color, these are books that children really want to read—books to excite their imagination, expand their interests, make them laugh, and support their feelings. With fiction and nonfiction stories that are high interest and curriculum-related, All Aboard Reading books offer something for every young reader. And with four different reading levels, the All Aboard Reading series lets you choose which books are most appropriate for your children and their growing abilities.

Picture Readers
Picture Readers have super-simple texts, with many nouns appearing as rebus pictures. At the end of each book are 24 flash cards—on one side is a rebus picture; on the other side is the written-out word.

Station Stop 1
Station Stop 1 books are best for children who have just begun to read. Simple words and big type make these early reading experiences more comfortable. Picture clues help children to figure out the words on the page. Lots of repetition throughout the text helps children to predict the next word or phrase—an essential step in developing word recognition.

Station Stop 2
Station Stop 2 books are written specifically for children who are reading with help. Short sentences make it easier for early readers to understand what they are reading. Simple plots and simple dialogue help children with reading comprehension.

Station Stop 3
Station Stop 3 books are perfect for children who are reading alone. With longer text and harder words, these books appeal to children who have mastered basic reading skills. More complex stories captivate children who are ready for more challenging books.

In addition to All Aboard Reading books, look for All Aboard Math Readers™ (fiction stories that teach math concepts children are learning in school); All Aboard Science Readers™ (nonfiction books that explore the most fascinating science topics in age-appropriate language); and All Aboard Poetry Readers™ (funny, rhyming poems for readers of all levels).

All Aboard for happy reading!

To my granddaughters, Kelly and Brittany,
with love—J.H.

For Bill, my city slicker sweetie—M.S.

Text copyright © 2004 by Joan Horton. Illustrations copyright © 2004 by Melanie Siegel. All rights reserved. Published by Grosset & Dunlap, a division of Penguin Young Readers Group, 345 Hudson Street, New York, New York 10014. GROSSET & DUNLAP and ALL ABOARD POETRY READER are trademarks of Penguin Group (USA) Inc. Printed in the U.S.A.

Library of Congress Cataloging-in-Publication Data

Horton, Joan.
 I brought my rat for show-and-tell / by Joan Horton ; illustrated by Melanie Siegel.
   p. cm. — (All aboard poetry reader. Station stop 2)
Summary: A collection of poems about school, including "Cafeteria Food," "Mrs. Hall's Instructions for the Class Picture," and "What I Tell the Bully."
 ISBN 0-448-43490-3 — ISBN 0-448-43364-8 (pbk.)
 1. School children—Juvenile poetry. 2. Education—Juvenile poetry. 3. Schools—Juvenile poetry. 4. Children's poetry, American. [1. Schools—Poetry. 2. American poetry.] I. Siegel, Melanie, 1961– ill.
II. Title. III. Series.
 PS3558.O698I3 2004
 811'.54—dc22

                              2003015058

ISBN 0-448-43364-8 (pbk)   A B C D E F G H I J

ISBN 0-448-43490-3 (GB)   A B C D E F G H I J

I Brought My Rat for Show-and-Tell
and other funny school poems

By Joan Horton

Illustrated by
Melanie Siegel

Grosset & Dunlap • New York

Table of Contents

I BROUGHT MY RAT
FOR SHOW-AND-TELL

I brought my rat to show-and-tell

For everyone to see,

But when I stood before the class,

He got away from me.

This caused a big commotion

As he scurried all about.

Kids were jumping up on chairs

And some began to shout.

"Calm down," the teacher hollered.

"Enough of this, I say."

Just then my rat raced at her;

She fainted dead away.

I brought my rat for show-and-tell.

I made a big mistake.

I'll never bring my rat again.

Instead, I'll bring my snake.

CAFETERIA FOOD

Wednesday is spaghetti day.

I bought a heaping mound,

And right before my very eyes

It started wiggling 'round.

Through the sauce the pasta crawled,

I stared in dumb surprise

To find it staring back at me

With two big meatball eyes!

I think this food is pretty weird.

What's more, I have a hunch

That every Wednesday from now on

I'd better bring my lunch.

HOW TO DO
YOUR HOMEWORK

Open your notebook and lie on the floor,

Prop up your feet on the chair.

Look at the first set of questions,

Complain the assignment's not fair.

Cover your pencil with bite marks,

Admire the pattern they make,

Doodle all over your paper,

Decide that it's time for a break.

Call up a kid in your class,

Brag that you got a tattoo.

He'll tell you he doesn't believe you,

Pretend that it's perfectly true.

Jump up and down on your bed,

Get bored and pester your brother.

Threaten to give him a noogie,

Stop when he yells for your mother.

Shine a flashlight through your fingers,

Figure out why they turn red.

Think about tackling the questions,

But play with your Game Boy instead.

Make up a dozen excuses,

Pick out the very best one

To give to your teacher tomorrow

When she asks why your homework's not done.

1. ~~Dog~~
2. StomaChache
3. Viking plunder
4. Broken lamp
5. Flood

BRENDA

On Monday, Brenda tweaked my ear,

On Tuesday, she stomped my toes,

On Wednesday, she kicked both my shins,

On Thursday, she socked my nose,

But Friday was the darkest day

Of my entire week.

That's when Brenda grabbed me

And kissed me on the cheek.

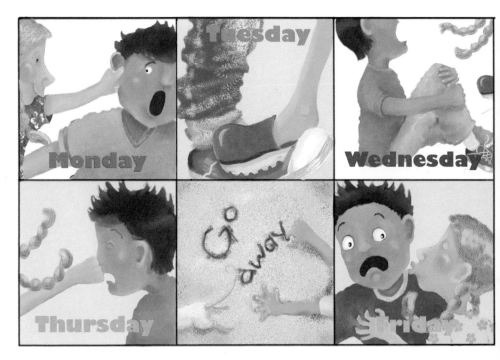

THE CLASSROOM PARTY

As fast as he could, Lumpy Orr

Was wolfing down cupcakes galore.

What happened next

Left the janitor vexed

And Lumpy with room
for lots more.

MRS. HALL'S INSTRUCTIONS FOR THE CLASS PICTURE

"Randy and Zack, tall kids in back,

Christy and Brian, change places.

Harvey and Heather, move closer together,

Darius, stop making faces.

"Kelly and Blair, smooth down your hair,

Ronnie, stop wrestling with Ned.

Sarah, don't fidget.

What is it, Bridget?

<u>Who's</u> making ears on your head?

"No bubble gum, Kate,

And stop shoving, Nate.

Honestly, you are the limit.

Geraldo, I know

That you gotta go,

But couldn't you hold it one minute?

"The photographer's ready,

Uncross your eyes, Freddy,

Everyone smile and say,

"Jenny Lynn Prime,

This isn't the time

To pick at the scabs on your knees.

"Let's try again.

What happened to Ken?

Randy, move back to the rear.

Thank goodness," she said,

With a shake of her head,

"Class pictures are just once a year."

THANKSGIVING PLAY

Mrs. Hall assigned us parts

In our Thanksgiving play,

The one our class is putting on

Tonight for the P.T.A.

I hoped I'd be a pilgrim

Just like Jeffrey, Sue, and Grant,

Or else the friendly Squanto

With his gift of corn to plant.

But when I saw the part I got,

I groaned, "Wow, what a bummer.

Why can't we skip November

And fast forward right to summer?"

But here I am in costume.

Mrs. Hall says I look perky.

I only wish I weren't the one

She picked to play the turkey.

POETRY ASSIGNMENT

I'm having a terrible time,

I never will learn how to rhyme,

There must be a gimerick

To writing a limerick,

I can't even think of one line.

SNOW DAY

"Hooray, hooray! Hooray, hooray!

It snowed last night; no school today."

Cheers ring out all over town

As girls and boys jump up and down,

But the loudest cheer of them all

Is from their teacher, Mrs. Hall.

CHRISTOPHER'S MATH TEST

Eight pears plus three more is ten,

Twelve minus nine equals two,

Take one dozen apples from six dozen more

And the total is still quite a few.

Seven times seven is seventy-seven,

Five into thirty is four,

These are the answers he put on his test

And zero was Christopher's score.

NAME _Christopher_

= 10

② $12-9=2$

1 DOZ

= 54/

④ $7 \times 7 = 77$

⑤ $5\overline{)30} = 4$

WHAT I TELL THE BULLY

So what if you are mean and tough

And trip kids in the hall,

And have the biggest muscles—

I'm not scared of you at all.

You're a dweeb, a dork, a dufus,

A gigantic ugly pox,

A reject from the planet,

And you smell like stinky socks.

NAME _Christopher_

= 10

② 12−9= 2

1 DOZ

= 54/

④ 7x7= 77

⑤ 5⟌30 = 4

WHAT I TELL THE BULLY

So what if you are mean and tough

And trip kids in the hall,

And have the biggest muscles—

I'm not scared of you at all.

You're a dweeb, a dork, a dufus,

A gigantic ugly pox,

A reject from the planet,

And you smell like stinky socks.

You walk like a gorilla

With your knuckles on the ground,

And, fungus face, you'd better not

Try pushing <u>me</u> around

'Cause your brain's a whole lot smaller

Than those cooties on your head.

That's what I tell the bully

When I'm safe at home in bed.

HARVEY

I'm not as good at playing ball

As Michael, Chris, or James,

So no one ever picks me first

When choosing sides for games.

When teaming up for spelling bees,

Kids look at me and pass

Till I'm the only one who's left

In our entire class.

I'm in the slowest reading group,

I lag behind in races

As other runners beat me

By at least one hundred paces.

I hope some day when I grow up,

I'll come in first, not last.

Meanwhile, I am hoping

That I grow up really fast.

HOMEWORK PAPER

When he saw my homework paper,

Dad was positively sore.

"An F in math?" he bellowed

With a loud, resounding roar.

He was madder than a hornet,

He was in a purple rage

As he paced about the kitchen

Like a tiger in a cage.

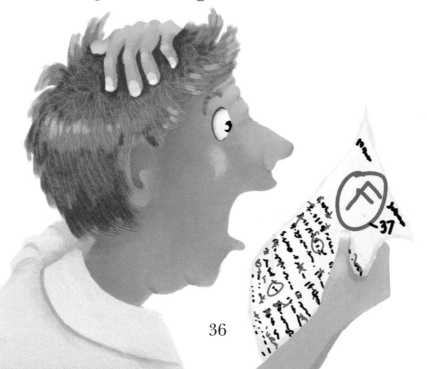

"For the life of me," he hollered,

"I don't see how this can be.

Why, I was always good in math,"

My dad reminded me.

When he saw my homework paper,

Dad was seething to the core.

I guess this means he'll never

Do my homework anymore.

VALENTINE'S DAY

They're passing out valentines.

Tasha's got two

And Cindy and Caitlin

Have got quite a few.

There's another for Simon

And several for Jenny,

A big one for Marcus

And three more for Kenny.

And here's one for Tina,

A red heart with lace,

The one that she sent

To herself—just in case.

ANSWER PLEASE

Whenever I'm bouncing clear out of
my chair,

Eagerly waving my hand in the air,

The teacher pretends I'm not even there.

But if she asks, "Where is Kalamazoo?"

And I don't know the answer and haven't
a clue,

I can count on her calling
on you-know-who.

So here is my plan. Starting today,

I'll simply behave in the opposite way.

If I'm sure of the answer, I'll make myself small

And if I'm not, I'll sit really tall.

PRINCIPAL'S
INTERCOM ANNOUNCEMENT

Girls and boys, attention please.

Good morning. This is Mr. Pease.

The math test scheduled for today

Is canceled and I'm pleased to say

I'm now excusing everyone

Who didn't get his homework done.

For those of you who buy your lunch,

Instead of beans and cabbage crunch,

They're serving chocolate cake supreme

With triple ripple fudge ice cream.

And one thing more before I go.

There's something all of you should know.

Tomorrow, there'll be no more school.

Only kidding.

April Fool!

THE MONSTER
IN OUR CLASSROOM

The monster quickly gobbled up the
letters A-B-C,

Then polished off the alphabet, including
X-Y-Z.

"A most delicious meal," he sighed,

And settled back quite satisfied

Till B-U-R-P gave a shout

And hollered, "Hey you, let us out."

The monster murmured, "Pardon me,"

Then opened wide and set them free.

BUBBLE GUM RAP

Blew a bubble, didn't stop,

Bigger, bigger, bigger—pop!

Teacher turned, saw the bubble,

Heard the pop, double-trouble.

Quickly blew one bubble more,

Bigger than the one before.

Started floating off my chair,

Past the teacher, through the air,

Soaring skyward with my bubble

Far away from double-trouble.

Teacher gasped and cried, "How weird!"

Right before I disappeared.

The End